LUMBERJACK

BY NICK GORDON

TORQUE™

BELLWETHER MEDIA · MINNEAPOLIS, MN

Are you ready to take it to the extreme?
Torque books thrust you into the action-packed world
of sports, vehicles, mystery, and adventure. These books
may include dirt, smoke, fire, and dangerous stunts.
WARNING: read at your own risk.

Library of Congress Cataloging-in-Publication Data

Gordon, Nick.
Lumberjack / by Nick Gordon.
    p. cm. -- (Torque : dangerous jobs)
Includes bibliographical references and index.
Summary: "Engaging images accompany information about lumberjacks. The combination of high-interest subject matter and light text is intended for students in grades 3 through 7"--Provided by publisher.
ISBN 978-1-60014-780-7 (hardcover : alk. paper)
1. Loggers--Juvenile literature. 2. Logging--Juvenile literature. I. Title.
SD538.G577 2013
634.9'8--dc23

                                                 2012007663

This edition first published in 2013 by Bellwether Media, Inc.

Printed in the United States of America, North Mankato, MN.

TABLE OF CONTENTS

CHAPTER 1

TIMBER!

The roar of a **chain saw** and the smell of freshly cut wood fill the air of the **logging camp**. Lumberjacks attach steel cables to a giant tree. Suddenly, something cracks. A cable has snapped. The lumberjacks scramble to get out of the way!

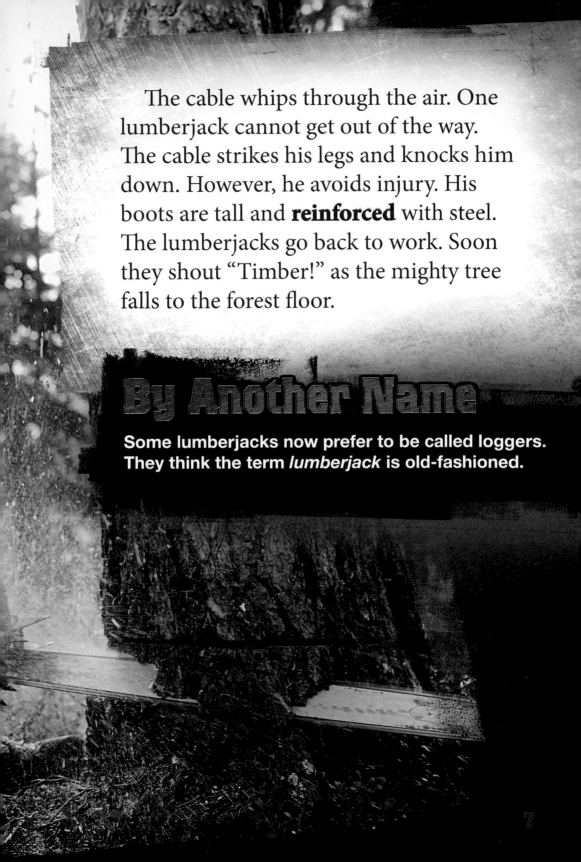

The cable whips through the air. One lumberjack cannot get out of the way. The cable strikes his legs and knocks him down. However, he avoids injury. His boots are tall and **reinforced** with steel. The lumberjacks go back to work. Soon they shout "Timber!" as the mighty tree falls to the forest floor.

By Another Name

Some lumberjacks now prefer to be called loggers. They think the term *lumberjack* is old-fashioned.

CHAPTER 2

LUMBERJACKS

Lumberjacks cut down trees to gather wood. Sometimes they must climb tall trees to do their job. Powerful chain saws allow lumberjacks to cut down the trees. Logs are then transported to the roadside and loaded onto **log trucks**. The trucks take the logs to a **sawmill**.

From the Air

Some lumberjacks are specially trained to use helicopters to find, trim, and move trees. They are called heli-loggers.

Beginning lumberjacks receive on-the-job training. Experienced lumberjacks teach them how to safely climb trees, fasten cables, and operate heavy machinery. Every lumberjack fills a specific role.

A Lumberjack Crew

Faller	**Cuts down trees**
Bucker	**Trims tops and limbs of fallen trees and cuts trunks into proper lengths**
Choker	**Hooks steel cables around bucked logs so they can be hauled out of the forest**
Equipment Operator	**Uses heavy equipment to cut down and move logs**
Chaser	**Tells equipment operator where to drop logs and unhooks steel cables**
Grader	**Inspects logs and decides how they will be processed**

Lumberjacks need a lot of equipment. Helmets, leather gloves, **chaps**, and steel-toed boots help keep them safe. Climbers use strong lines and **harnesses** to scale trees. Heavy-duty chain saws rip through tree trunks.

A Steep Job

Many logging machines cannot be used on steep mountains and hills. Trees in these areas have to be cut down by lumberjacks on the ground.

Some lumberjacks use large machines to cut and transport trees. **Harvesters** pull down trees and cut them into logs. **Swing machines** help lumberjacks load logs onto **forwarders**. Then forwarders haul the wood to log trucks.

CHAPTER 3

DANGER!

Lumberjacks are always in the path of danger. They can fall from trees or get hit by falling limbs. A large tree that is cut in the wrong direction can crush anyone in its way.

Equipment is also dangerous. Harvesters can pull down trees on top of lumberjacks. Swing machines can drop logs on them. Lumberjacks driving log trucks always risk a **fatal** accident on the road.

The steel cables that lumberjacks use to take down and move trees can cause serious injury. They can snap if they are pulled too tight or hooked incorrectly. A cable that snaps often whips out at a very high speed. It can easily cut off an arm or leg.

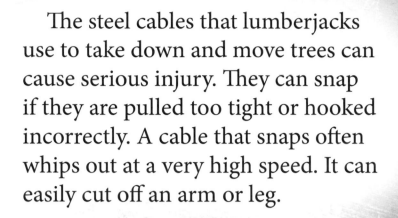

A Grave Number

In 2010, nearly 60 lumberjacks died on the job.

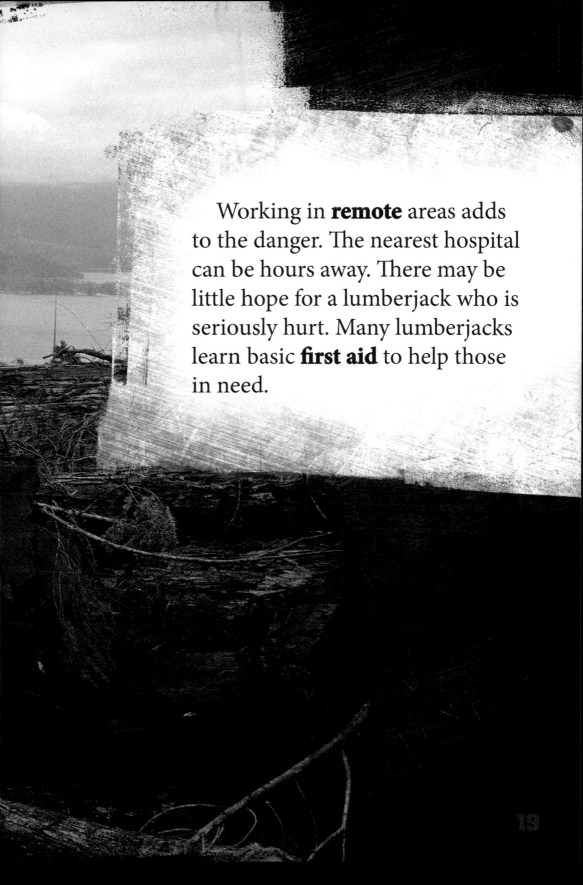

Working in **remote** areas adds to the danger. The nearest hospital can be hours away. There may be little hope for a lumberjack who is seriously hurt. Many lumberjacks learn basic **first aid** to help those in need.

Lumberjacks work hard for many hours at a time. They must always stay alert and aware of the trees, machinery, and other lumberjacks. Most do the job because of the pay and their love of the outdoors. However, they all know what they risk with every trip into the woods.

Tragedy on the Job

On August 27, 2007, two Tennessee lumberjacks died in separate accidents. Junior Hamby was struck in the head by a falling tree limb. Russell L. Griffith was riding on a piece of machinery when he fell off and was run over. The two accidents occurred only three hours apart.

Glossary

chain saw—a power tool that uses teeth on a spinning chain to cut through wood

chaps—strong clothing worn over a lumberjack's pants; chaps are strong enough to stop a chain saw from cutting into a lumberjack's leg.

fatal—causing death

first aid—emergency medical care given to a sick or injured person before he or she reaches a hospital

forwarders—large vehicles that pick up and haul fallen trees out of the woods

harnesses—straps that connect lumberjacks to ropes or lines for climbing

harvesters—large machines that pull trees to the ground, cut off their limbs, and cut the logs to size

log trucks—large trucks that transport logged trees

logging camp—the location where a lumberjack team bases its operations

reinforced—made extra tough by using more materials than normal

remote—far away from populated areas

sawmill—a building where logs are cut into usable lumber

swing machines—large machines that pick up and load logged trees

To Learn More

AT THE LIBRARY

Bateman, Teresa. *Paul Bunyan vs. Hals Halson: The Giant Lumberjack Challenge!* New York, N.Y.: AV2 by Weigl, 2012.

Flatt, Lizann. *Life in a Forestry Community*. St. Catharines, Ont.: Crabtree Pub. Co., 2010.

Reeves, Diane Lindsey. *Scary Jobs*. New York, N.Y.: Ferguson, 2009.

ON THE WEB

Learning more about lumberjacks is as easy as 1, 2, 3.

1. Go to www.factsurfer.com.

2. Enter "lumberjacks" into the search box.

3. Click the "Surf" button and you will see a list of related Web sites.

With factsurfer.com, finding more information is just a click away.

Index